MY CUT-OPEN PALM: UKRAINIAN POETRY IN TRANSLATION

MY CUT-OPEN PALM: UKRAINIAN POETRY IN TRANSLATION

Translated into English
by Oleksandr Fraze-Frazenko

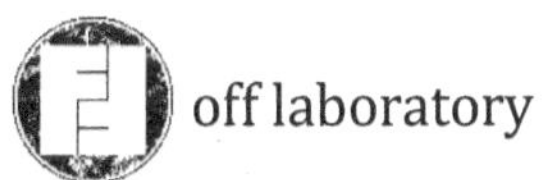

Lviv. New York. Pittsburgh
2026

Cover design incorporates a decorative element from *Magistri Pauli Crosnensis Rutheni Sapphicon de inferorum vastatione et triumpho Christi* (Kraków, Florian Ungler, after 31 March 1513). Courtesy of the National Library of Poland (Polona).

Designed by the author.

Published by the OFF Laboratory.

www.offlaboratory.com
www.frazefrazenko.com

Library of Congress Control Number: 2026905651

ISBN 979-8-9949518-1-1

INTRODUCTION

Poetry is your blood and flesh. Not the food you eat, not the water you drink. Poetry crawls into all your cracks, poetry pounds its stream into your temple. And when you give the greatest oath of your life, you cut open your palms with a knife and press hands together so that your blood may mix. That is how poetry spreads. This book is my cut-open palm, which I extend to you, reader.

Most of the poets in this book had a decisive influence on me and on the signposts of my life. When I was a child, my grandmother, Countess Panina, had a rather extensive library. True, it mostly consisted of Soviet editions, which of course bore the red imprint of party censorship. These were mainly Russian translations of world classics, as well as multi-volume editions of Lermontov, Chekhov, and others. In our country house she also kept an enormous collection of the Soviet magazine *Foreign Literature*, where they published anyone at all — from Pablo Neruda to Jim Morrison. That was my first reading.

Later, when I was already in gymnasium, I somehow got hold of a textbook from an experimental Ukrainian literature curriculum — I didn't exactly get it, it simply ended up in my hands somehow. It was designed for a twelve-year school system, and this was the volume for the twelfth grade, at a time when we only studied eleven. So there was no way I would ever study from this book officially, but in it I encountered authors who changed my life completely. The most important was Ihor Kalynets, one of the greatest Ukrainian (Halychynan) poets of the twentieth century (his foreign equivalents might be Paul Éluard or Czesław Miłosz), a poet who spent half of his poetic career in Siberian camps and exile, a poet whose court sentence contained nothing but lines of his own poems about longing and love.

That textbook turned my life around.

Then, in the somewhat smaller library of my other grandmother, Ahafiia, I discovered complete collected works of Ukrainian classical writers — Pavlo Rusyn, Hryhorii Skovoroda, Ivan Franko, Lesia Ukrainka, and many others. There was also a multi-volume *History of the Ukrainian Insurgent Army*, though that is already beyond the topic of poetry.

All this reading laid the foundation and pushed me to begin writing like the poets I read. Later I had the honor of becoming friends with some of them. The most important friendships were with the already mentioned Ihor Kalynets, the avant-garde rock poet Viktor Neborak, whom I met through the legendary translator of poetry Andrii Sodomora. It was Sodomora who took me by the hand and led me behind the curtain of the translated text — it was then that I began to immerse myself in the incredible world of translation, this surgical work with fragile transplants.

At first this led me to translating my favorite poets from English into Ukrainian: the Restoration-era poet Earl John Rochester (2007), and also my scandalous bestseller of selected poems by the already mentioned Jim Morrison (2013). I never even dared to imagine translating anything into English — it was not simply unreachable, it did not even exist on the horizon.

In 2015 I was on an impossible mission — to travel to New York and make a film about the New York Group of Ukrainian poets. When this miracle finally happened and I crossed the ocean both ways, there arose the need for subtitles for the film *(An Aquarium in the Sea, 2016)*, whose world premiere was to take place the following year in the United States. That was when I first encountered translating Ukrainian poems into English. Other translators helped me, but I began to read already familiar phrases in the words of another language, and it felt strange. Around that time I remember sitting on a bench in the upper part of Kościuszko Park in Lviv, looking down from the hill at the twisted paths and the dense green lungs above me, when lines of my own poem, written several years earlier, began to spin in my head — but I heard them in English, and I started writing them down. On that bench I translated an entire cycle: five of my sonnets about a phantom woman and a snake in the folds of her dress.

That is how it all began.

Now I myself am in exile, like most of the poets I admired all these years. Perhaps if I had read something else, my life would have unfolded differently. But here — here is my outstretched hand. I have already cut a thin strip across my palm with a knife. Roses are growing from it.

I extend my palm to you.

Oleksandr Frazé-Frazénko

** Viktor Neborak, Oleksandr Frazé-Frazénko, Andrii Sodomora*

PAVLO RUSYN OF KROSNO

(1470–1517) was one of the earliest known poets connected to the cultural world of Halychyna (now Western Ukraine) and a representative of Central European Renaissance humanism. Writing in Latin, he studied and later taught at the University of Kraków, where he signed his works "Paulus Ruthenus," affirming his identity as a man of Rus' — a medieval East Slavic cultural and political tradition whose name was later appropriated by Muscovy and transformed into the modern term "Russia."

His poems explore the dignity of the poet, the passage of time, and the promise of immortality through words, forming one of the first bridges between the medieval world of Ruthenia and the emerging literary culture of Renaissance Europe.

EPIGRAM ON POETRY AND TIME

Time devours all things —
cities, kings, and marble monuments.
Only the word escapes its teeth.

What iron cannot guard,
what stone cannot preserve,
the poet saves with a line.

So let death claim the body —
it cannot touch the voice,
which travels farther than the grave.

HRYHORII SKOVORODA

(1722–1794) was a philosopher, poet, and wandering teacher, often called the "Ukrainian Socrates." He rejected official positions and worldly success, choosing instead a life of voluntary poverty, traveling from village to village with only a flute, a Bible, and his manuscripts. His poetry and parables revolve around the idea of inner freedom and the search for one's "kindred work" — the calling that matches the soul's true nature. An enduring legend tells that he composed his own epitaph in advance: "The world tried to catch me, but did not succeed."

The Hryhorii Skovoroda National Literary and Memorial Museum in Kharkiv region was destroyed by a direct Russian missile strike on the night of May 7, 2022.

Григор. О^{с} Σ.

SONG 20 FROM THE GARDEN OF DIVINE SONGS

He whose heart is pure and bright,
Whose soul is cleansed of hidden stain,
Needs neither helm nor mail for fight,
Nor girds himself for war or pain.
His stainlessness his armor is,
His innocence a diamond wall;
God is his shield, his sword, his all.

O world! O witless, faithless throng!
Thy hope in kings and crowns is cast.
Thou think'st thy shore secure and strong?
A whirlwind sweeps away such dust.
Purity — behold thy Zoar's height!
Innocence — heaven's court of light!
There take thy rest, there lodge aright.

That holy city fears no flame,
No slander's shaft, no cunning mine;
Unburned it stands, untouched by shame,
Unshaken by the storm's design.
Purity — that adamant;
Innocence — that city blest.
There dwell in peace, there make thy rest.

Within that city foes are loved,
And good for evil is repaid;
For others' health their own is proved,
Not friends alone their kindness made.
Where stands that city fair and broad?
Thou art the city — purge the fraud,
Cast out the poison — temple of God.

TO EVERY TOWN ITS CUSTOM AND ITS LAW

To every town belong its custom and its law,
Each head is ruled by its peculiar mind;
Each heart for love and warmth its longing draws,
Each throat its own delight in taste doth find.
But I am held by thoughts that will not cease —
One thing alone denies my spirit peace.

One Peter crawls for rank at noble doors,
Quick-handed Fedir cheats in trade and gain;
One builds his house in newest foreign forms,
Another traffics — weigh his fraud and feign.
But I am held by thoughts that will not cease —
One thing alone denies my spirit peace.

One spreads his fields without a bound or end,
Another breeds strange cattle from afar;
Some train their hounds for hunts that never mend,
Some keep a house that roars like revels' jar.
But I am held by thoughts that will not cease —
One thing alone denies my spirit peace.

One twists the law to suit his cunning art,
A student's skull with disputations rings;
Some burn with Venus' fever in the heart,
Each has his fool that round his temples clings.
But I have but one care beneath the sun:
How I may die with reason clear and one.

I know that Death, like scythe in sweeping hand,
Will neither crown nor sceptre pass aside;
To Death it matters not what rank may stand —
Like fire in straw, it swallows all in stride.

IVAN FRANKO

(1856–1916) was a poet, writer, and public intellectual, one of the founders of modern Ukrainian literature. Born in a blacksmith's family in Halychyna, he rose from rural poverty to become a central cultural figure of his time. In his youth he embraced socialist ideas and was repeatedly imprisoned by the Austro-Hungarian authorities. Later Soviet cultural policy selectively appropriated his legacy, emphasizing his early radical writings while simplifying and heavily editing the complexity of his views.

Despite his deep knowledge of contemporary European literature, Franko remained skeptical of early Ukrainian modernist movements, favoring instead a literature grounded in social responsibility and national development. A remarkably prolific author and translator, he worked with many European literatures. In his final years he suffered from a debilitating illness that left him unable to write by hand, yet he continued dictating works until his death in 1916.

WHY DO YOU COME TO ME IN DREAMS?

Why do you come to me
In dreams?
Why do you turn to me again
Those wondrous eyes so bright, so deep,
So sad —
Like wells whose water sleeps in coldest depths?

Why are your lips so mute?
What blame, what pain,
What unfulfilled desire
On them, like crimson flare,
Ignites — then sinks again
In night?

Why do you come to me
In dreams?
In life you spurned and wounded me,
You tore my heart and left in it
Only those loud lamenting cries —
My songs.

In life you do not know me still.
You pass me on the street — you pass;
I bow — you never turn your eyes,
You never nod your head,
Though well you know — you know too well —
How madly I have loved you,
How through long nights I suffer,
How year by year I press
My grief, my pain, my songs
Deep down within my heart.

Oh no!
Appear to me, bright star,
At least in dreams!
In life I must forever pine —
Not live.

Then let this heart, worn out by care,
Like pearls cast into mud,
That fades and withers, dries away —
At least at sight of you in sleep
Revive again,
Beat stronger in its sorrow,
Breathe freely, like a human being,
And taste that golden miracle —
That youthful happiness,
That longed-for, fearful,
Sinful bliss.

PRISON SONNET 22

A figure entered. "What is your name?" — "Franko."
"Hm, Stanko?" — "Franko!" —
"Stanko — write it down.
How long here?" — "A month." —
"Hm! And you, my love?"

— "Seven days." — "And you?"
— "I leave tomorrow."

He noticed a book. "You're allowed to read?"

— "Yes." — "Hm." He glanced
At bunks, at ceiling. "Hm-hm! No vent here?"

— "None." — "None? Hm. Good. Write that down."

The turnkey rushed in:
"There are vents in both the punishment cells!"

— "In both? Write that down!
And you might open a window here."

(Perhaps the stench struck his nose.)

— "Our window stays open day and night."

— "Ah. Hm. Write that down." And they left.

HAUSORDNUNG

Outside, there, beyond the prison fence,
There is a constitution, certain laws;
For us they are only a darkened myth,
A bell whose ringing no one knows the source of.
The whole constitution, the entire law
With us are simplified beyond all measure:
There exists but one code in the criminal ward,
And that strange code is called *Hausordnung*.

It is not written down, yet it exists
Only in oral and fist-borne transmission;
Through practical lessons the prisoner learns it.
Its decrees are swift as relays.
The director, the turnkey, the worthy guards —
They are its experts, executors, and interpreters.

ANIMA SALTANS*

In plush and gauze, in rosy powder,
With hair let loose in sign of mourning,
On the brow
A shadow of melancholy,
In the breast a heart,
Pierced by the arrow of secret sorrow,
And on the lips
A mysterious whisper —
Like reproaches, like love incantations,
Like the unconscious babbling of a child.

In the eyes, a dull gleam of fatigue,
In the voice, a chilly softness,
Pretentious coquetry —
Thus I glide,
With the rustle of silk,
With the movements of a half-sated serpent.

Thus I spring up,
Like a cuckoo from a someone else's nest,
I spread my arms —
A symbol of despair,
I choke on wild weeping —
And I leap, stamp, whirr, laugh,
Spin on one foot,
Alluring, unforgettable, zephyrous,
Thoroughly sensual,
And always ready to chatter nonsense —
Anima saltans.

—

** Latin: "the dancing soul."*

THE STONECUTTERS*

I still was young — life smiled on me and burned,
Love blossomed bright, hope flowered in the spring;
And suddenly a wonder came and turned —
I fell into a sleep so deep, so stern
That death seemed reaching out her hand to cling.

I slept so fast and hard. My friends drew near,
Looked long at me, and said: "He now is gone."
They ran for priests and carpenters — and here
Made all prepared, the funeral feast set on —
The priest shut fast the coffin — I lived on.

I slept so deep! I did not hear them sing
Above me their sour, hopeless funeral cry;
I did not hear the earth in thudding fling
Beat on the coffin as it fell from high,
Nor felt the seal of the eternal vow — all passed me by.

—

** For as long as the poem has been known to readers, "The Stonecutters" has existed without its first three stanzas. Ivan Franko crossed them out in the earliest autograph (No. 216), and they were never published in his lifetime or in subsequent standard editions. I encountered these suppressed stanzas in the 50-volume academic edition of Franko's works, where they are reproduced from the manuscript. However, the deleted stanzas are highly significant. They describe a scene, which closely parallels the structure of a Masonic initiation ritual — "initiation into the Masonic Order." In such rituals, the candidate undergoes symbolic death, darkness, confinement, and rebirth into a new moral and communal identity. Read in this light, the suppressed opening reframes the entire poem: the dream of the stonecutters becomes not merely a social or political allegory, but also a symbolic narrative of initiation.*

I saw only a dream: as if before me
An endless plain — immense, empty, and wild;
And I stood there, chained fast with iron fetters
Beneath a towering granite cliff — while onward
Stood thousands just the same as I.

On every brow life and sorrow had carved furrows;
In every eye love's burning fire still burned;
Each pair of hands was wrapped in chains like serpents,
Each pair of shoulders bent and sagged below —
For one great weight was crushing all alike.

In every hand a heavy iron hammer,
And from above a mighty voice like thunder roared:
"Strike at this rock! Let neither heat nor cold
Hold you back! Endure the toil, the thirst, the hunger —
For you are destined here to break this stone."

And all of us, as one, raised up our hands;
A thousand hammers thundered on the stone;
In thousand shards the splintered fragments scattered,
Rock chips flew wide — and with the strength of despair
Again and yet again we struck its stony brow.

Like waterfall in roar, like battle's bloody cry,
Our hammers thundered, blow on blow;
Inch after inch we forced the ground;
Though many there were crushed and maimed by rock,
Still we went on. Still nothing stopped us.

And each of us well knew that no fame would be ours,
No memory among men for this bloody labor;
Only then would people walk upon this road,
When we had broken it through and leveled it —
When here beneath it our bones had rotted.

We never longed for human glory's praise,
For we were neither heroes nor strongmen.
No — we were slaves, though freely we had taken
The chains ourselves; we became slaves of will:
On progress' road we were but stonecutters.

We all believed that with our own hands
We would break the rock and shatter granite,
That with our blood and with our bones
We would build a hardened road — and after us
New life would come, new good into the world.

We knew that far away, in the world we left
For labor, sweat, and chains,
Mothers and wives and children wept for us;
That friends and foes alike, bitter and wrathful,
Cursed us, our intent, and all we did.

We knew it — often our souls were in pain,
Our hearts tore, and grief pressed on our chests;
Yet neither tears nor sorrow nor the body's burning pain,
Nor curses pulled us from the work —
No one released the hammer from his hands.

So we go on, all of us bound in one community
By a sacred thought, with hammers in our hands.
Let us be cursed and forgotten by the world!
We break the rock, we clear the way for truth —
And the happiness of all will rise upon our bones.

BOHDAN-IHOR ANTONYCH

(1909–1937) was a poet associated with the literary life of interwar Lviv. Born in the Lemko region (then part of the Austrian province of Halychyna), he studied at Lviv University and wrote primarily in Ukrainian.

Antonych's poetry combines symbolism, pagan and Christian imagery, urban modernity, and a distinctive mythopoetic vision of nature and technology.

He died in Lviv at the age of twenty-seven. His work, only partially recognized during his lifetime, later became central to the Ukrainian modernist canon, largely due to the efforts of poet Ihor Kalynets, who during the Soviet period searched for Antonych's destroyed grave, worked to restore his legacy despite the risk of persecution, and later established the Antonych Prize for poetry.

CAROL

Carpenters are hewing silver sleighs,
A snowy road lies spread and white.
On those sleighs into unknown blue
They will carry the Child of God.

Carpenters are hewing silver sleighs,
Dreams of spring begin to gleam.
On those sleighs the Radiant Lady,
Eyes like those of a doe.

The sun walks in a fur cap,
The Slavic Child lies asleep.
The sleighs move on, the Lady weeps,
Life is spreading out like snow.

DEAD CARS

Like fragments of shattered stars, on the graveyards of machines lie frozen cars asleep, the red blossoms of rust measure years and minutes stiffened into copper, and only an unknown solar core sways, like an eternal truth, which too is unknown and just as elusive to us as the blue spirit of gasoline.

It happens that people, like jackals,
disturb in anxious sleep
these metal corpses, spreading out the wares of
their desires, thirsts, and needs as in a market,
and the dead bodies, in the blueness of nights,
become sinful beds
for homeless lovemaking of buffoons and
prostitutes, into whom the stars of evil
pour their fumes.

As we dig up the bones of reptiles
beneath the cliffs of forgotten ages,
one day they will dig up, in the graveyards
of our cities, these metal bones.
Girls with nameless flowers,
palms bearing bread, green rue,
and new cities with squares of azure,
where fiery lions roll.

But restless shadows, unquiet ghosts
rise from beneath the earth,
from beneath the squares, from beneath the grass.

Metropolis, with the palms of your red walls, lay to rest the winged souls of cars!

BALLAD OF THE BLUE DEATH

Phantom tenements and courtyard sheds,
like thickets of darkness, narrow and wet stairways,
the abyss of night no one has measured, the sorrow
of dark gates and the languid breath of mold.

A crumpled, stained scrap of paper,
a short, simple note: "No one is to blame.
Do not search for the culprit!" In quiet bast shoes
the moon goes along the roofs like a wise cat,
decay drifting.

From exposed wires blue vapor rises like a bouquet,
from copper, swollen veins blue blood streams.
Behind the wardrobe, half-asleep, shivering in fear,
a phantom solo on the clarinet of sorrow —
do you hear?

The blue current burns like a soul in inspiration,
and the whisper of madness rocks two hearts
from the bottom of consciousness.
And night into a furious whirl! And with blue
blossom gas into the torn carpet of silence!

Onto the bed — a boat of luxury and the tedium of
love — a moon-mouse sits, cynical and stunted, and
body with body, tightly entwined for the last time,
twists in insatiable spasms of pain and pleasure.

Bent above them, the blue angel of gas
crowns them with blue fire like myrtle,
and their souls, like lilies, he casts into ecstasy
until they burn away like the final drops of alcohol.

TRUMPETS OF THE LAST DAY

Hundred-storied tenements sleep
like weary little beasts,
geographers draw stars in chalk upon
the map of the sky,
in the ruddy glow of lanterns
raindrops drift like winged sand,
and the moon lies on my couch like a golden cat.

Dead fish rust in pools, coal and roses blacken,
merchants and naked girls,
prisoners in jails and poets.
An orchestra of policemen blows melancholically
into trumpets and horns
while the bourgeois god
counts stars, souls, and coins.

Beneath the city live, as in fairy tales,
whales, dolphins, and tritons
in thick black water like tar,
in terrible cellars below,
phantom ferns, griffins,
and drowned comets and bells.
— O forest of stone, what will you do
when a new flood sweeps you away?

VADYM LESYCH

(1909–1982) was a poet from Halychyna whose life and work were shaped by exile, rupture, and long periods of silence. He began publishing in the late 1920s, but early in his career he became involved in a literary controversy when Bohdan-Ihor Antonych — one of the most important Ukrainian modernist poets of the interwar period — accused him of plagiarism. The episode deeply affected Lesych, and he withdrew from literary life.

For many years afterward his whereabouts and activities remain largely unknown; he effectively disappears from the historical record during the turbulent decades surrounding World War II. He later re-emerged in the Ukrainian émigré community in the United States, settling in New York, where he lived a quiet, largely private life while working outside literary institutions. His mature poetry, marked by symbolist imagery and philosophical introspection, reflects memory, war trauma, and the fragile reconstruction of inner life after historical catastrophe.

TO BEGIN AGAIN

To begin again
from a... b... c...
And when will it be time
to end again?

A fragment from my emptiness
fell upon me like a stone.
And I cast it, destined by fate,
into the flight of the unknown —
into the wings, broken
in shattered space.

There is only one solitude:
and that one
lies beyond us.
Then it will remain
as though we were no more.

PARCHMENT OF MEMORY

The parchment of memory is crumpled —
it does not even rustle,
as the darkened gardens of evening hiss,
and the wind bends the arc of distance like a bow,
and the meadows rejoice beneath the violets of
dusk.

Brown smoke — and a rounded, globe-like
emptiness.
Smoke from the clumsy skeletons of life,
now turned to ash.
An emptiness waiting to be filled.

The parchment of memory is rusted.
It lights the candles on the altar of evening.
Like polar moss, the frost turns blue.
It trembles beneath the white stars;
Grieg's music trembles like a spider's web.

Things completely unrelated, existing
each for itself,
like ripe fruits from different trees,
fall heavily in the silence of the garden
onto the earth fading in anticipation.

The shadows become like trees,
and the trees become like shadows.
The parchment of memory rustles
with the sand of broken mirrors
in the scattered desert.

AN EPITAPH IN THE SAND

I have become a memory to myself.
Anxiety still flutters, but it has no wings.
Where can one return when there is no return?
And the roads are like rivers dried up in the desert
beneath a yellow sky.
The sand does not quench thirst —
it only fills your eyes.
The wind will sweep away
the footprints in the sand,
and I walk without direction.
I walk. And I see:
somewhere in the distance
the sun's fire burning
behind the towers of sand,
behind the sand of towers.
I remember the sun rising like fire —
and the journey.
Anxiety sank into the towers of sand.
I became a memory to myself,
a troubled monument
made of sand
beneath a yellow sky.

WE MUST PLACE STONE UPON STONE

We must place stone upon stone.
Words must be gathered from the desert whirl.
From the abyss of the eyes we must draw
the pink transparency of mornings,
and the graying depths of memory.
You must stack brick upon brick.
You must rake the ferns from the moss.
You must build: hew logs for cabins,
bind the beams
from the howling wind
that heats the trees and rages with sand.
You must cross out the empty space.
And for the quiet birds,
tossed by the wind between earth and sky,
you must weave nests from brushwood.
And to see a man's joy —
to touch it with fingers,
with clusters of cooled flowers, with lips,
to feel the warmth flowing through the body.
To be entwined in the hair of nerves,
to close your eyes,
and see, see clearly
through the tightly shut eyelids
how the structure is growing —
between the whispers of words
fluttering unspoken
in flocks of birds,
between the quarries of hearts
on the rails of a green morning.
This will be the first day.

CATHARSIS OF WAR

They are cut down in shadows in the wind
of wings turned to dust,
on the steps of the fading color of silence
the abysses of wounds are healed:
early, early, in the morning, the fortune teller,
ravens playing their game, no turning back,
early, early, early, in the morning...
A tiny seed...

I begin again with words,
that I have forgotten the meaning of, their scent,
I have forgotten the color... I have forgotten... I have
forgotten...
I have forgotten who I was.

I begin from the stove, from the gate,
my mother's fingers, my father's hands, the warmth,
the piano, the broken violin,
from the palms, soft and crumbling like ashes,
from faces that have blurred like oceans,
sealed with the dew of the sun
in halos of tears of washed-out rainbows,
from faces left behind, gone,
unnamed neighbors,
the closest ones who have sailed out of reach
into the universe,
became the farthest, the most distant,
and then are gone.
"Ashes... warmth... body burning...
to Canaan let us go.
I begin with Jonah, Ivan, Ivas, Iasochka,
ashes, sycamores, sunflowers,
from the sun,

though I see places deserted,
damp, overgrown with tares;
severed heads like broken watermelons,
spinning in the ditches;
lost eyes, gouged out, sockets rinsed,
muddled, blind, twisted;
and the smoke of the roads on their hands and lips,
in their hair, I see a shadow: we are them.
Fingers bent, crosses of bodies,
souls are smoke on the horizon,
the days are gray, grayer than gray,
covered with mist,
without gilded frames, without silver-edged
sarcophagi;
our landscape is a torn void,
the blood of plowed twilight
a close memory.
Hosanna...

YEVHEN MALANIUK

(1897–1968) was one of the central figures of twentieth-century Ukrainian poetry and a leading voice of the émigré literary tradition. Born in the Russian Empire (in present-day central Ukraine), he served as an officer in the army of the Ukrainian People's Republic during the struggle for independence after World War I. Following Ukraine's defeat, he spent the rest of his life in exile, first in interwar Europe and later in the United States. After Malaniuk left Ukraine, his later works were long rejected in so-called mainland Ukraine; only the militant poems written during his time on Ukrainian territory remained widely known.

Meanwhile, his poetry deepened significantly and turned inward. His later work, as well as that of Lesych, was strongly influenced by the much younger New York Group of émigré poets. Often called the "emperor of iron stanzas," Malaniuk's poetry combines classical discipline, philosophical reflection, and intense historical consciousness.

His work is marked by themes of national catastrophe, exile, cultural responsibility, and the moral burden of history, making him one of the most powerful and influential Ukrainian poets of the twentieth century.

AVE CAESAR

Ave Caesar, singing August,
Most-August ruler of years!
The sweetness of late fruits grows bitter,
Your radiance more and more intolerable
For the earth, almost blinded.

Ave Caesar, still your day shines
In the colonnades of groves, on the forum of fields;
Your Rome is soaked with a bottomless blue —
It dissolves in it and slowly vanishes,
And like a vision flows into song.

Ave Caesar, frozen upon the throne,
You are already statue, marble, mark;
Only the sun still plays in your crown,
Only your temples are silvered with blue —
Burned by the wind of years.

OVER THE ATLANTIC

With a cold fire
an alien, superfluous autumn.
Only at times a familiar wind breathes —
to fan the autumn glow.

A familiar wind, as if entirely one's own,
native — from Kherson, one might say.
And a steppe day appears in a vision:
a garden, Jacob's ladders, and mother.

A saddened father, a wise grandfather,
my dear brothers...
Where are you?
Autumn and autumn. The trail fades.
Above the waves — only gulls.

FROM THE DIARY

Autumn here is not called "Indian summer"
for nothing.
Indeed, October is in full bloom
With pink gold upon the greenery of the
imperishable,
Like a second May. Of course, it is completely
different,
Unseen, unspoken, unreal,
Perhaps even a little wild.
The day
Bathed in a truly summer sun,
Hot as the tart, belated passion
Of an old man who has already known
The early spring that never blossomed,
The stormy summer in flashes of lightning
And August, treacherously tightened
By drizzling rain...

And the nights are a bit stifling,
Reflecting all the charm of autumn's constellations,
That burn like cold diamonds
On the dull warm velvet of the sky.
And there is something frantic in it.

And so this first experience of a strange
Indian summer lasted a long time,
And with it something grew and endured,
Something that was also new to me.

You called it "friendship."
And I am still afraid to call it
That which has no name, no name
In poor and incoherent human language.

PARASTASIS*

I

The coffin sprouts roots —
The roots sprout from the coffin.
The snow will melt,
And the snowdrops will sprout.
And then the grasses.
And in May,
In May the branches will bloom
And you will be
— the wind,
— the breath of the earth,
— the song of the blue,
As you have always been,
As you have been all my life.

** Memorial service in the Eastern Orthodox Church.*

II

And now the snow is falling on the posthumous
flowers. The snow lies like Your blanket.
And lies still.
Not far away are churches, crosses, trees.
And at night the wind blows miserably.

"It is I, the sleepless one.
I cry for You.
It is I, inconsolable,
Watching your sleep
And unraveling its strange cause.
And I can neither unravel nor guess.

...In Vietnam, strangers are leaving
a desert behind them.
In Congo, they are reuniting Katanga with bombs,
And poor Chombe in Paris
is waiting for Petliura's end.
And the storms are roaring across the Atlantic,
And the United Nations are stitching up the wounds
of their borders —
The wounds of the borders,
that run through the living body,
separating the head from the heart
and the heart from the genitals...

...How good it is that You cannot hear it,
cannot see it, and you do not even care,
Because there is no time:
Death is the great universal,
cosmic loneliness,
But it is also a great cosmic
crooking of the spirit.

III

I betray myself
— for You, for You.
You see, I no longer write
in a poor man's iambic pentameter,
The iambic pentameter of youth.
There is no rhythm or rhyme,
My heart has lost its rhythm
and no longer feels
the consonance of rhyme.

It tugs at the veins
with a racing,
torn pulse.
It suddenly stops sometimes,
And in those pauses I hear
— Your presence.

Then I take
a little nitroglycerin:
The explosive material
to produce silence.

But I know that at some point
the nitroglycerin will not work.
The pavement will expand
into a great silence.
Before the date.
— Forever!

BOHDAN RUBCHAK

(1935–2018) was a poet, literary critic, and scholar from Halychyna, and a leading member of the New York Group of émigré poets. Born in Western Ukraine, he was displaced during World War II and grew up in postwar Europe before eventually settling in the United States, where he became a professor of literature and an influential interpreter of modern Ukrainian poetry. His verse is marked by refined modernist technique, mythological imagery, and philosophical reflection on memory, eros, and exile.

Known for his rigorous self-criticism, Rubchak often published his poetry in small private editions, giving copies to friends and readers while later burning down unsold ones in his backyard — a practice he described as an expression of uncompromising artistic standards and the precarious conditions of Ukrainian literary life in exile.

In the last decade of his life, he also became widely known for his sharp and often unsparing presence on Facebook, where he regularly engaged in polemical critiques of contemporary Ukrainian literature and its institutions.

A REMINISCENCE OF THE MOON

—

When I touch your face,
my fingertips open with the blossom of an apple tree,
and the moon above us
lives the life of a saint.

Then a pure sky
opens up in me,
and you touch it,
like the wind in May.

—

But one day it will come,
the moon that was our friend
and with a malicious touch
will turn our happiness into dry sand.

And we will still take it in handfuls
and pour it from one greedy hand into another,
searching in vain for that near miracle
that has been with us
for so long.

We will still gaze together into the pools of rivers
and into the pools of our hearts,
until we are overwhelmed
by the cold realization of the futility of our efforts —
until we realize
that everything is dead to us.

And then we will say goodbye
with an embarrassed, slightly confused smile,
and walk away from each other —
strangers.

—

Somewhere beyond the suns there are dreams,
and in them there is moonlight.

—

Rounded memories hang
on the branches of silence, ripening
like plums. I know:
Ishtar has left you,
and you are an empty garden,
where the white statues of loneliness
are like the white of death.

—

A question touched the lips.

—

No, not now.

In the farthest star
the diamond body of death glitters,
and the festive gestures of the days obscure
the consciousness with a living haze
of the thousandfold multiplied reflections
of your face. But remember:
one day you will see it again and again.

it will be framed by shining blades,
and your gaze
will turn into two pillars of salt,
and your powerless gaze
will search in vain for your own pupils.

—

When
the mirrors of tears fade in my pupils,
when the leaves of my palms turn black,
when
the last fruit falls from my brow
and autumn's gray hairs are in my temples,

be with me then.
Be with me then,
when there is nothing but
a big empty white moon,

and nothing else.

Then
love
me.

—

Be close to me.
We will reach the farthest reaches of existence,
the rocks against which
the waves of feelings crash,
to a land where the vast expanse of water
merges with the moonlight,

where unnecessary movement does not obscure the vibrations of the universe,

where every leaf —
from everything
a sap flows into us that gives us
absolute steadfastness.

Where in the moonlight
the shadows
of our past blur.

—

You will raise the relics of the moon
in your hands
to my lips.
I will kiss them away,
and they will light a steady
fire in my soul.

It will become a statue:
Surrounded by
summer, winter, spring,
fall, summer, winter,
spring,
and it will still burn.

And everything that touches it,
even for a minute,
will turn into columns and trees.

—

The moon
with its rays
changes the world like the eyes of a child.

—

The moon — yes. The moon knows
even the winds,
even the stones.

The light of the moon
cannot divide bodies
and hides
dreams and quiet shadows.

The light of the moon
builds white lines,
and you enter
into memories from the farthest reaches.

The light of the moon
cannot judge deeds,
though it carves
the paths of fate in the palm of its hand.

The light of the moon
cannot divide bodies,
though it can
sting your temples.

The moon can. The moon knows.
The moon is alpha. The moon is omega.

—

Give the moon everything:
all your pain and all your joy,
and the love that grows strong on the sun-baked earth,
and the loaf of bread for working hands,
and a child's prayer,
and a pregnant silence, and an embarrassed singing,
and the calm gaze and the tranquility of cemeteries,
and the lakes and the clouds —

give everything to the moon,
to the cold moon.

—

The moon
decorates the cliffs,
in the stone
whispering its sleep,
and in the stone
images of the distant past are born.

—

Lonely girls
wear the stigmata of the moon on their breasts —
two reflections of its face
filled with greedy suffering,
when the night is
filled with unbridled thirst
they drink its fullness.

And then
the full moon burns
in their golden locks,
and their white thighs
are its bedrooms.

—

Now comes the thing
that we dared not dream of:
that radiance,
so pale and white.

It's like a moon's circle
flying unstoppable toward my face,

like the moon
is penetrating
deeper and deeper,
deeper,
deeper into your pupils.

—

The moon — yes. The moon knows.
The moon is alpha. The moon is omega.

SONG FOR MARYANA

This love is like rare autumn fruit —
Late-ripened, deep;
Like night that trembles, soft and mute,
In its last sleep.

This love I carried out of September
For a bird's wild grace,
And for the blue whispering embers
Of your calling face.

For hair that flows across your breast
Like threads of rain,
For palms that shine in moonlit rest
With sacred flame.

In this love I live as in a garden
Old and dim with mist,
Gathering silvered joy that glistens
In shadowed leaves.

I lost myself within your face
As in strange land;
Within its secret, quiet space
I seek who I am.

VASYL STUS

(1938–1985) was a poet and dissident born in the Donbas region, widely regarded as one of the most important Ukrainian poets of the twentieth century and a central voice of moral resistance against Soviet totalitarianism. Arrested twice for his dissident activities, he spent most of his adult life in prisons, labor camps, and internal exile, where he continued to write under conditions of extreme isolation.

Much of his poetry survived only because fellow prisoners memorized and later reconstructed his texts after manuscripts were confiscatedStus died in a Soviet prison camp in 1985. Although officially recorded as heart failure, many contemporaries and scholars believe his death was the consequence of sustained persecution and camp brutality.

Today he is regarded as a symbol of spiritual integrity and the unbroken will of Ukrainian culture.

OH HUMAN

oh human, I cannot believe your life
is only about staring into my cell.
Doesn't your own life call you? I beg you, tell me:
have you at least somehow found your path,
serving in this joyless place
where everything is filled with human torture?
you always stand beside my heavy sorrow,
and I can feel your pain in the way you stand,
because you are twice as sad as I am.
I have myself — and you are only a shadow.
I am the good; you are dust, decay.
we are both prisoners — that is what we share:
on either side of this door, I am here, you are there.
we are divided by these walls of law.

THERE GROWS A WALL

there grows a wall between the world and the soul.
play hide-and-seek so they will not recognize you
through layers of deadly memory,
through numb thoughts and ice floes of the senses.
spurs have sunk into such a frozen soul.
unwillingness only shortens the desire
to seek those wells where the world
endures forever —
to recognize you and to kill you
with all its irresistible deadly weight.
there is a wind that blows souls out of bodies,
breaks trees, bends grass along the way,
and even creates a multifaceted emptiness
exhausted by its own perfection.
such sadness everywhere — how many
fates are lost, how many carried on
to the final breath, the final moan,
to death. such sadness everywhere,
where the wall grows between
the world and the soul.

WE ARE YOUR LOVERS

we are your lovers already, death.
life shines for us only through the fog.
you should rejoice for now, my dear,
while the sky's fields are sown till dawn.
crimson music roams here
on the sharp crest above.
a cuckoo cries, drunk with tears,
calling "cuckoo," because she knows how.
we drank the juice of birch tonight,
we drank the river's water.
long-limbed sycamores downriver
were slowly crunching in the ice.
and swida was about to burn,
pyrola rolled through the snow.
the earth rose sharply in the ravine —
she felt the fruit as though it were a sin.
how good it is, close to the forest,
to lose the meadow path somehow,
to fall backward into the open sky —
like a baby in a cradle.

YOU HOLD A CANDLE

you hold a candle above your head
until your hand grows almost tired —
not for the night, but until you're dead.
the timid darkness: no more fire.
bats fly like bullets through the night,
my cheeks are frozen stiff with fear.
I cannot see you, cannot hear —
how can you live without the skies?
those sleepy creatures lift their eyes:
you are not the one resurrected.
an owl cries, echoing in the niches,
and Dante wanders here, neglected.
little black thing, my pointless beauty,
I'll be your target — will you shoot me?
the candle does not even blink.

THERE IS THIS SILENCE

there is this silence. silence. dry and black.
gray doves draw circles in the sky.
you turn to fortune-telling — why
is the night wrapped so deeply in darkness?
I think I even see nimble soothsayers
throwing cards before you in quick succession.
your faith is bound to blank and gloomy victims —
they obey without question, without escape.
a candlestick sleeps. a candle sleeps within it,
already flattened — a butterfly, an acanthus.
amid all this, your pain is like a diamond,
the blinding eye of your despair. rise.
do not wipe the gunpowder from the candle —
it is only your fear that you cannot master.

INTO THE DARKNESS

into the darkness of my sleep I go.
the bitter waters of oblivion rise.
the edge draws nearer, so I look
into the emptiness of days and years
and wonder where that edge lies —
from which all lost souls return
back to the beginning,
down to the valley of that fragile beauty
spreading everywhere with fresh young blood.
where are you going with these reckless steps?
you begin to know yourself — relentless path —
and still you follow someone else's footprints.
the thin strip of years keeps narrowing the way.
it is like your shadow walking toward you:
it knows your future, and already
it has broken this path of yours —
abyss and darkness. the end.
to step beyond is too hard for us,
to live with this uncertainty —
as if, halfway through a step,
your foot hangs frozen in the air.
half-desire,
a wavering cut in two —
you see the margins of the hills of patience,
you see the invisible spaces between them.
oh God — what if those spaces reveal
how small we are?
what is one mountain to another?
what can we do?
endless time stretches between us,
those weary distances of life,
when inspiration fades to shadows,

when storms of passion burn themselves out
after filling our lives so suddenly.
I want to go beyond time.
I want to begin this life again.
I want to witness the beginning.
why should I wait until I die?
the hills of fate, the highlands of the cry,
that first cry breaking through —
shattering the certainty of numbness and decay.
oh those unbearable surges of being,
those relentless attacks of fear,
that daring will to escape oneself,
that will to burn alive to death,
that frozen patience waiting,
that feeling never enough.
move on, move on, boundless forces —
you are young, your inner pain drives you forward.
your effort alone sustains you,
pushing you to dream of tomorrow.
and then you fall — it feels like death.
and then you suffer as never before.
you are a tiny flower in the wind.
oh uncertainty, my companion —
I take the road where hearts will meet.
my heart is yours, your blood is mine.
let us hear the birds tonight,
hear how earth meets sky at that line.
close your eyes — the secret
is about to open for you.
do not be afraid. do not run.
I know how hard it is
for us to heal this pain.

THE WHEELS

the wheels, the wheels, they strike the road —
like a ferry striking a wave.
hey Charon, here we are, my friend,
we bring some laughter and pain.
the wheels strike, the wheels strike,
they roll us somewhere else.
we'll never go back home again,
we'll never see that place.
the wheels, the wheels, they strike the road,
the wheels, the wheels, they strike —
oh Jesus, oh Lord, and all the gods,
and all the goddamn filth.
and Moscow, and Bear Hill,
and everything we pass —
this is our prison road,
swollen with our tears.
and Vyatka, Kotlas, Ust-Vym,
to Chibyu we are driven.
this is the Prison Union Land,
the land that God forgot.
forgotten by the Devil too —
another god is ruling:
a Marxist, racist man-eater
with a gaping mouth.
from Moscow to Chibyu we go,
to the internment camp —
that's how we build the future
again with blood and bones.

I WANT TO DIE

I want to die so badly!
I cannot be silent,
I cannot be crying.
one last lightning —
I want it this morning,
to rise for the final time.
this day will end it —
I will wait for it and die,
and never come back.
the deepness of peace,
the silence will lull,
a song will grip
my heart one final time.
I cannot breathe.
I just want to die.
all dreams are gone,
all thoughts are gone,
all laughter is gone,
all colors — gone.
it yawns like a chasm,
this vertical path.
I cannot climb it,
cannot even look.
I feel I cannot —
my body is all pain.
it tightens my throat
into a single scream.
let the sound lift me —
I just want to die.
I cannot endure,
I cannot wait.
the abyss is there,
patience is here.

I suffer so terribly —
oh God, let me die!
or simply disappear:
to die in these screams,
to fall into fragments,
to flow with the wind,
to vanish in time,
snatched from the soul
into the nameless.
the hills of destiny have passed,
snow covers everything.
I cannot see the road.
the blizzard rages.
my mother's hands —
I saw them this morning —
hang in the air,
searching blindly
for the ghost of her son,
the birthmark on his face,
his bent, shrunken shoulders.
I just want to die —
to slip away unnoticed
beyond hope,
beyond the horizon of endurance,
beyond the walls of prostration,
behind bars of rage,
behind fences of fury,
behind vines of screams,
behind the spikes of obsession —
to lie down
in the silent snow
somewhere among the mounds
of the missing souls.
I want to die so badly!

YOU WANT TO ESCAPE DESTINY

you want to escape destiny? impossible.
the thunder strikes — your life is gone.
and here you stand, like a nightmare made flesh:
the death of life, the life of death.
what can I do? at least I will try
to test the gold of love —
will those who love you stay beside you,
no matter what?
will they recognize you still,
you — after all that life?
will they be afraid of what
you have become?
oh please — how can I know?
life moves along its strange path;
those winds have carried you away.
yet you endure — my faith, thank God:
the stronger the wind,
the less you fear it.

IN THIS BLUE FIELD

in this blue field, as blue as flax,
you are alone, and no one else around you,
and suddenly you`ve seen someone pass,
one hundred shadows, blue as flax.
and in this field, as blue as flax,
you had to be alone, just lonely,
to realize your fate is a redemption,
in this blue field, as blue as flax.
one hundred shadows start to grow
all of a sudden they are like the woods
they start to go just toward you.
oh should I run? what should I do?
or should I stay? that`s right, I think I`ll stay.
and only here, only in this field,
as blue as flax, I`ll be enslaved right here
don`t feel like home in here anymore,
in this blue field, as blue as flax,
you are alone, one hundred are against you,
and each of them is filled with grief,
and each of them will never stop
to curse you like you never heard before,
like throwing stones at you, and every word
is burned with loneliness of yours
and finally you`re going slightly mad
in this blue field, as blue as flax.

WHAT ARE YOU WAITING FOR

what are you waiting for — tell me, what?
is someone coming at this early hour?
is there someone you long to meet?
and if there were — would you believe it?
there is a dead end in the inner world.
there is a woman, heavy with thought,
whispering: God bless this place,
oh God, bless this goddamn place.
I see a distant, foreign land:
a field, a burning viburnum tree,
and a grave. Ukraine is weeping
over her son's head: farewell, my son.
two of your enemies try to weep —
how hard it is for them to imitate grief.
they are only glad he never loved
Ukraine, her land, her skies — not at all.
she mourns for him; her shadow bends,
and emptiness spreads beyond the field.
and in all you hear
echoes of frozen depths
tonight.
oh evil demon — whom
do you curse, and curse, and curse?
whom do you call within yourself?
your broken fate? a fragment of warmth
beneath the ashes of those times?
whom are you waiting for? you do not know.
you will wait until you say: enough.
you give. you take.

BE PATIENT

be patient, patient — for patience grinds you,
your spirit turns to steel, so be patient.
no one will save you from your trouble,
and no one will change your mind.
hold to your path — keep it to the end.
the world may end; you will stand last.
whether the highway leads to hell
or the stairway rises to heaven —
stand firm, do what you must.
go your way — the way you chose,
the way that chose you forever.
it began when you were a boy:
God Himself commanded it.

IHOR KALYNETS

(1939–2025) was one of the central voices of twentieth-century Ukrainian poetry and a key figure of the cultural revival known as the Sixtiers movement. Born in the Lviv region (Halychyna), he emerged in the 1960s with a distinctive poetic language that united modernist experimentation with deep roots in folklore, Christian symbolism, and historical memory.

In 1972 he was arrested by Soviet authorities during a wave of repression against Ukrainian intellectuals and spent nine years in labor camps and Siberian exile. Much of his most powerful poetry grew out of this experience of imprisonment, inner freedom, and moral resistance. In 1987 Kalynets publicly declared that he was no longer a poet but only "a poet's press secretary," saying he would return to writing poetry when Ukraine became free.

Although independence came, he never resumed poetic writing, devoting himself instead to cultural work, public life, and the support of younger generations of writers.

FREE-VERSE VERDICT 17

to renounce the metaphor
crucified
on newspaper pages

hanged
on the gallows of the airwaves

dried
between the press of covers
of swollen books

fingered over
in conversations
like the last loose woman

to renounce
even the very metaphor
about it

but in no way
can I rid myself
of the day-before-yesterday's dream

where I, blood-soaked,
defeated
without any hope
a great beast

look —
they gave no prize
to the gapers

the defeated one
has your face

who then is he
to you

to renounce the metaphor
is to renounce
not only —
oh not only —
the dream

FREE-VERSE VERDICT 18

having hauled the wind
from a white sail
like a fish from nets

having pulled from the eyes
of a stranger
a splinter
of unguessed longing

having robbed the beloved
of her sleepless dream

having uprooted
from the wild field of the soul
yet another stump
of illusion

not bypassing,
with conceit,
the baroque arsenal
of publicistic rhetoric

having pressed an ear
to the wall of the day
like to a prison cell

having plundered
faded flowers
from the herbarium of a dictionary

having cut off,
in the meadow of metaphor,

the head of a thistle
and a flowering fern

having rounded the phrase
after the model
of the full moon

having written for myself
a free-verse
verdict

three times a day
I convince myself:

if you are not
an informer
against the poet,

then what are you,
poetry?

NIGHT WITHOUT TENDERNESS

"Night is tenderness."
— Fitzgerald

Reality: black snows claw toward the eyes
while instead of sand they sift snow
today flared toward spring like a Bengal fire
weary, I sink beneath a blanket — the coffin lid
but how to rid myself of this clearing of sight
when the weighted sun tilted its stem
know: the sky you would wish to lean toward flees
beyond thin stars
I hold my breath deep inside
so as not to blow away your presence

Plea: save me from the great time
the immeasurable space the great noise
the great solitude the great bedroom
from a thousand eyes long arms
give me something small
like myself

Reality: melody,
frightened by the long night,
curl into a gray mouse

into the keyhole slit
make your way out of the body of the dead
p i a n o

look —
through the reed-thin opening
the moon pours a glass
long-washed stains

of wine on the table

long ago the arguments
have flowed out
of these walls
like from a broken jug
in the nap of the carpet
live
absorbed whispers

the cobweb on the candlestick
is not of paraffin —
real

Awareness: night without tenderness,
you came and you will depart

in submission I learn
the stale hardness of bread
and the hardness of the world
to the final threshold

unable to weigh
a speck of tenderness

a Hoverla for memory —
night is tenderness

Illusion: you have just come out of the foam of waves
and lay upon the river of your hair
I do not ask who you are,
woman

here my hair floats down the river to the sea

today it is black upon gold
yesterday it was light upon gold
tomorrow it will be golden upon gold

Illusion: tell about the lips —
pink from fever
white from fever
worn from sighing
full from sin

once I stood beneath them
a golden apple tree
that did not shed

to my happiness

Illusion: and the eyes will tell —
in them will be unhidden
colors of the elements — sky sea sand

and only the little men in them —
memory of me —
all will recoil from them

people crave mirrors,
not memory

Illusion: if now I confessed to myself, then
not the retreating wall of ebb
rolling back toward the horizon,
not the blanket of reddish sand,
not the porcelain sky of the sea,
but a hollowed stone of the Renaissance —
or more than that:
old bogged pinewoods,

a fern that never bloomed

Unknowing: where is your home —
a bus every day, a sea in a shell —
I have a forest pink in early spring,
a green autumn forest, a lonely forest,
a little house covered by a dream
by two playing cards

Elegy: the beloved fell as a tear into the sands

Unknowing: can you
cut off the wings of womanhood,
the wing of motherhood,
for the sake of a true arrow shot
as a one-breasted rider —
can you

Reality: flowers,
strange flowers
that still wished to die
for people's confessions of love —
those flowers from the Halytsky market
also died for my love,
and I do not even remember
their name

Plea: spring will not return, and summer
tends my poor little garden.
Sit at least at the edge of my heart,
for I have something to beg of you:

gild my autumn,
gild my lonely garden,
give the garden abundant fruit,

and the fruit enduring seed,

rejuvenate my wintering —
enter my garden at night,
leave in the snow sparse traces —
traces of lingering love.

Long elegy: blue vegetation each day openly
blooms above us — ripening
the fruits of longing for wings,
for the formula and metaphor of worlds
where our only and fitting
by the ribs of suffering is driven into the run —
a feeble word of half-truth
hangs from pale lips in a half-voice,
the company lies sleeping in rows
amid the grass of hard reality,
amid the pacification of fragile radiance.
the wife became a tear in the sands,
and all the brothers-in-arms to a distant face —
almost with my lips someone speaks
that the longest road of becoming human
in this most perfect of worlds,
revived from deadness by the rib of suffering,
it is a honeycomb of feelings
like white from the spectrum, like the silence
of a prayerful night from the sounds
of a great scale.

Night is tenderness

Awareness: the beloved will become
a tear in the sands —
I will wish to find my brothers-in-arms;
they will have one cold face.

the woman who carried me in her womb
will bear shame in her heart.
only one endures submissively —
the homeland I barely felt with my foot —
this is mercy.

Reality: all tongues mingle —
the language of honor with baseness
in a Babylon called soul —
and the feeble word of half-truth
hangs from bloodless lips
in a half-voice.

Reality: a miserly scrap of light
she tears from herself,
gouges out the eyes,
feels above,
feels from within,
drinks from the lips
the barely warm stream of a sigh,
the mosquito squeak of stars
cuts off,

and whispers to every nerve:
beyond me there is no one sweeter.

from the last illusion she robs
with black f l e s h —

darkness

Dream: take sleep from me —
a brief flash;
take the memory of sleep —
long for a whole life.

two in one face,
two in my heart,
once in the bridal wreath,
once in thorns,

two in one face,
two in my heart,
spear, do not sleep — strike true,
blood from beneath the rib,

two in one face,
two in my heart,
night in the midst of day — OTHER —
three nights of death,

why die before death?
rise at once —
two in my heart,
two in one face,

they rose from perishable decay,
the crucified dead rose —
two in my heart,
two in one face,

two in one face,
two in my heart,
again in the bridal wreath,
again in thorns.

Last plea: only to gnaw through
the hard fists of sleep.

the iceberg of morning is struck out
from blue cold

in the window.

I am not an insect in amber.

I am in ice, in a frozen slab.

who are you
who reach toward me
with a finger,
with warm breath —

do not let me live out my age
with frost on my lips,
with bitterness in my heart,

without tenderness in the night.

night without tenderness
night without tenderness
night without tenderness

WIND

again there was wind

it drummed on the shutters,
jangled on the panes in a greenish clatter
like with teeth

it tore out tow
from between the logs,
sucked like a vampire
the spirit from the house

and from us — the coziness

again there was wind

it found every crack
for sand
that grits on the teeth
and in the joints

again there was wind
it carried off letters from books,
waves from the transistor
(hey hey wind from Ukraine)

it squeezed out tears,
clouded,
like the sun

EMPTYING OUT

little by little things depart —
first books, then clothes,
some trifles from the shelf

then the conversation broke off
when I woke alone as a finger

the cat almost a guest
(the frozen fish has run out)

here and there
the wall crumbles,
there are more spiders,
the stove has cracked

I give away
seeds of asters, dill,
the house spirit, dishes

a drowning man,
more and more often
I clutch at a volume
of Shevchenko

I grow less —
drop by drop
I send myself away

now tender, now indifferent, now irritated

and still an entire spring
lies ahead

PRAYER

I know (bitter is that knowledge)
neither the earth nor humanity
you will save

neither a country nor a people,
not even a single town
or village — you will save

not a forest,
a tree, a blade of grass,
an anthill — you will save

not a lake,
a water lily,
a cloud in the sky,
a fish in the water — you will save

not friends, mother, daughter,
not a single beloved face — you will save

for a long time I have wanted to renounce you,
to forget your name, after the period
to break the pen forever

but today —
not in general —
this night,
in this very hour,
me alone
you save

s a v e

IDENTIFICATION

Who signed it? Lechoń? Norwid?
Or the Siberian wind from the penal camps?
— M. Riechal, "Poet's ID Card"

on my identification

the moon has placed
a chipped seal

therefore it is not entirely visible

how a brother
takes a brother
on a pitchfork

here is my own fingerprint,
dipped in viburnum juice

now I cannot renounce
a single line
any more than my papillary lines

I cannot shield myself
with any armor
of a pseudonym

like a snail
I put out my horns
from every word

my recommendations
are of the highest respectability

first Antonych,
later Prosecutor Antonenko,
now Antonenko-Davydovych
corresponds with me

instead of a pen
a blackthorn serves me,

which the muse pulled out
of her pierced foot

I wonder how the PEN Club
could believe
in such a stylus

therefore my poems —
scratchings, graffiti,
in a single copy

on the heart

I wonder
how they were found
and awarded
the Franko Prize

after all, they are surely
not carved by stonecutters,
not eternal revolutionaries

just so —
prematurely withered leaves,

though viburnum ones

VERONIKA. A TEAR

To Natalia — friend of the Deceased

It is easier for me.
I did not walk in the mournful procession,
did not weep with a mother's weeping,
did not weep with an orphan's weeping,
with the weeping of the White World
over the black abyss.

Yet here is Your victory:
from such a distance,
and after so many years,
you press from my eyes my heart,
hardened in iron.

You are the White World,
the Bitter Palette,
the Golden Clay,
the Highland Inspiration,
and a wasted work.

And today You are my *threnos*,
blinded by the vision of the Hlyniany Tract,
the final road —
VERONIKA, TEAR...

Once more you bring victory,
you affirm victory
over the clay of Hlyniany,
over hardness.
You leave in your name
an unfading wreath,

you leave an unconquered charm
in the rough chamotte
of the candlesticks — horses
somewhere beneath the eaves of Lychakivska.

From the half-darkness
they carry out from the depths
the golden foil of light,
to illumine for us
the Perfect Face,
lately always living.

To illumine our misfortune,
and again return into decay,
leaving a barely perceptible
halo of light above the head.

In cemetery flowers.

I finish drawing
in your unfinished self-portrait
the quietest flower of the earth
with the loud name: VERONIKA. A TEAR...

I summon you
not with a trembling plate
at a spiritist table.

Now You are an Angel.
Be beside your orphaned ones
a gentle Breath.

I summon you
not from a triumphal arch
a Winged Nike,

but that one
met for the last time
in the old-town Market Square —
a tired woman
with a sorrowful confession
to me, an unnamed brother,
lost among centuries-old stone.

Behind your shoulders
I see slender Renaissance buildings.
They are wings that did not rise upward
but were pinned to the everyday,
to disillusionments.

To the earth,
robbed of the hot colors of Hlyniany carpets.
VERONIKA. TEAR...

Incredible —
yet then the goblet "Under the Lion"
was our last goblet.

Reality is a grounded lion, called to life
by the hands of our ancient brothers.
Which of those hands
supported in misfortune?

Only on the friezes
of petrified townhouses
Winged Lions remain —

lost Venetian lions.

And on the ceramic wall of the café
there will go and go

Young Lviv Women
beneath black umbrellas,
level with the singing towers
in the living sky —
nameless and eternally beautiful.

Then and Now
I summon from among them
one with a name: VERONIKA! TEAR...

It is easier for me:
I did not walk in the mournful procession,
did not weep with the weeping of the White World
over the black abyss.
Yet here is Your victory:
you press from my eyes
my heart,
my threnos.

She who brings Victory,
affirms Victory by non-being,
is no longer a Grave,

but a Root
of the quietest flower on earth — Veronika,
a Root in my tear,
a Root in our souls,
a Root from which will be woven
the Tree of Memory.

And this means:
our youth has departed.
Our Golden Winged Clay —
V E R O N I K A.

PARTING

One more night the sky will open to the Homeland,
one more time the rivers will lie on their backs,
they will not close their eyelids until there vanishes
from their pupils the most lingering of stars.

One more night.
Mother has finished digging potatoes,
she crosses her sleep, and in sleep,
not having lifted the crosses,
kisses the weary feet of God's Son,
so that her son's trace on earth will not grow cold.

One more night. A book lulls the daughter to sleep,
the walls have parted — her hand a little wing.
Fly your fill in dreams in the silvery gleam,
and find the Little Prince among the stars.

One more night. The wife has shut the window —
these flowers unbearable, unbearable, unbear—
no, these flowers came alive
in the night and grew sorrowful
for their Polovtsian, for their Scythian steppe.

One more night — not the first and not the last,
of the sweetest sleep, holy Homeland.
My beloved ones, good night —
and I am already dawning,
for I am already dawning in distant worlds.

VIKTOR NEBORAK

(b. 1961) is a poet, literary scholar, and cultural organizer associated with the late Soviet and post-Soviet literary revival in Halychyna. Born in Ivano-Frankivsk, he studied at Lviv University, where he later taught.

In the 1980s, Neborak became one of the founding members of the influential poetic group Bu-Ba-Bu (Burlesque–Balagan–Buffoonery), which played a key role in reshaping Ukrainian poetry at the end of the Soviet era through performance, irony, and linguistic experimentation. His work combines lyricism with urban imagery, theatricality, and reflections on language and identity in a transforming society.

Neborak's poetry also significantly influenced Ukrainian rock music of the late 1980s and 1990s, particularly through collaborations with musicians and the adaptation of his texts into songs within the emerging alternative and underground scenes.

I APPEARED IN SOMEONE'S DREAM

I appeared in someone's dream,
funny,
a year younger,
saying all the things
that are forgotten after waking —
or perhaps not saying them at all.

Quiet music was playing,
and the one to whom I came in a dream
understood everything without words.

It was not in our city.
It was once, in winter.
The streetlamps shone blue,
the light fell like snow.
And she, in her sleep, was smiling —
why are you so funny, why are you?
Please, don't come to me in dreams.
That is allowed to someone else.

That is all.
A small love.
There was no place for it in reality.
There was no true light for it.
Snow — and the sad streetlamps shining.

ROOM

I will be cheerful in the evening
because now I am sad,
she said —
the elusive mood of a person
who does not love you.

And I built this day
like a palace in the air,
filled it with caresses and words.
In every room there would be only us.

The room is blue, the room is pink —
come in. Look how I live.

How much I could give
on this day:
from your breath
a song would be created,
and people, hearing it,
would stop in the middle of spring.

And I would create like God.
You see —
all in beauty, in majesty,
I become human,
waiting for what you will say...

She will be cheerful in the evening,
watching a TV program
in her ordinary apartment,
in her ordinary beauty.

VASYL MAKHNO

(b. 1964) is a poet, essayist, and prose writer whose work bridges the cultural landscapes of Eastern Europe and the United States. Born in Chortkiv, Halychyna, he emerged in the late Soviet period as part of a generation that reconnected Ukrainian poetry with European modernism, urban memory, and personal historical experience.

Since the early 2000s he has lived primarily in New York, where exile, migration, and the dialogue between old and new homelands became central themes of his writing. His poetry often blends autobiographical narrative with historical reflection, exploring the fragile continuity of memory, family stories, and displaced identities.

Alongside poetry, Makhno is an influential literary essayist and cultural commentator. His work has been widely translated and is recognized for its philosophical lyricism, documentary precision, and deep engagement with the layered histories of place.

10

OUR LADY OF KRYVOLUKY

Stryjna brought news that the Mother of God had
appeared in Kryvoluky.

"This is the one," Grandma Anna explained to me,
"the same we saw in the church —
the one we lit every year with a wick of
burning straw
so she could escape to Egypt.
The Mother of God fled to Egypt with Joseph —
and we, at the Bazar, lit her way.
Every year she fled,
and every year we lit a candle for her."

We put the chickens in the barn
and hid an old rusty bicycle with one wheel —
the one Fedyo used to ride to school.
Now Fedyo was in the army,
and the bike had been dismantled for parts —
only the frame and the wheel remained.
Still, it was a pity, said the old woman,
looking up at the sky, waiting for rain.
She didn't really need rain,
because the house and its windows were covered
with dried tobacco
that we handed over to the collective farm
every year.

My grandmother took out her shawl
with the ruzhas,
put on a white shirt,
and took a patched bag
with which she used to go to the store for bread and
tomatoes.

She said we would drink water in the field
from a spring near the Chervona Kernytsia,
and stuffed into the bag
an empty vodka flask with a chipped neck
and some bread smeared with lard for a snack.

We caught up with Stryjna near the Chervona
Kernytsia —
she wore sandals and a colorful skirt,
carrying the same string bag and a handkerchief
where she kept the money.
After a while we passed the Kryvolutskyi end
and came to a field road
among larks, poppies, and burnt stubble
where the last eagles still walked
like paramedics.

It was a three-kilometer walk to Kryvoluky.
The old woman and her daughter kept talking —
about Jesus, praying,
exchanging news about tobacco and sweet potatoes.
From their conversation I learned
that a war would soon come,
that our Fedyo was already in the army,
that fish in the pond were floating belly-up,
that a plague had struck the chickens,
that man is mortal —
and all this was for our sins.

I was prevented from seeing the Mother of God
by several dozen women
singing pious songs
near the place with the icon and wildflowers.
We stood there for an hour —
I began to fuss and wanted to go home —

and my grandmother remembered the tobacco
that still needed to be brought to the barn.
It was already getting dark,
and the larks in the field,
swallowing the coolness of August, fell silent.

Finally the old woman said
that the Last Judgment was coming,
and Grandma agreed with her.

And I held on to my grandmother's hand,
afraid for our tobacco, chickens, and unicycle —
afraid that Fedyo would scold me
when he returned from the army.

Because I had traded that unfortunate wheel
for a pack of cigarettes.

ON THE BIRTH OF FOXES

A spring breaks through the soil — and a river
gives birth to a fox, and she runs.
The river rolls up its left sleeve,
and the fox's winter fat

will slacken, for she is looking
for a burrow, for field mice, for food.
She has to circle the mountain —
not easy with winter fat.

Meanwhile the river, its icy banks,
will flood with water and drown the gardens;
it will feel the fish wintering below,
their fins, and its own coolness.

So I leave the river to itself.
Somewhere apart, a flash of fur
will glimmer through a thin mist
and vanish quickly in the brush.

Whatever the river now may be,
whatever fox it may have borne —
gray as gray ash,
or red, just having dropped

along the shore a crimson shadow
from which the wings of hunger grew —
both the gray and the red one hear
that the ice has begun to move,

that they must watch the current,
must search for food,
because foxes, of course, from rivers are born —
and sometimes from poems.
Perhaps.

JURIJ ZAWADSKI

(b. 1981) is a poet, translator, publisher, and literary scholar from Ternopil, Halychyna, associated with the experimental strand of contemporary Ukrainian poetry. Emerging in the late 1990s, he developed a distinctive style that explores visual, phonetic, and digital forms of poetic expression, often focusing on the materiality of sound, rhythm, and language itself.

He is the founder of the independent poetry press Krok, which since 2009 has published Ukrainian and international authors and become an important platform for cross-cultural exchange.

Zawadski has a speech stutter, which he consciously transformed into a source of poetic expression. This experience led him toward rhythmic and phonetic avant-garde forms, where broken cadence, repetition, and acoustic texture often shape the structure of his poems.

MADE

I DON'T KNOW WHAT HAPPENED

Not with eyes you see me, not with eyes,
not with eyes you see me, not with eyes,
not with eyes you see me, not with eyes,
not with eyes you see me, not with eyes,
not with eyes you see me, not with eyes,
not with eyes you see me, not with eyes,
not with eyes you see me, not with eyes,
not with eyes you see me, not with eyes,
not with eyes you see me, not with eyes,
not with eyes you see me, not with eyes,
not with eyes you see me, not with eyes,
not with eyes you see me, not with eyes,
not with eyes you see me, not with eyes,
not with eyes you see me, not with eyes,
not with eyes you see me, not with eyes,
not with eyes you see me, not with eyes,
not with eyes you see me, not with eyes,
not with eyes you see me, not with eyes,
not with eyes you see me, not with eyes,
not with eyes you see me, not with eyes,
not with eyes you see me, not with eyes,
not with eyes you see me, not with eyes,
not with eyes you see me, not with eyes,
not with eyes you see me, not with eyes,
not with eyes you see me, not with eyes,
not with eyes you see me, not with eyes,
not with eyes you see me, not with eyes,
[...]
not with eyes you see me, not with eyes.

IN THE CHURCH

I don't know what happened.

Up, down —
a road through the mass of wet snow.
Not waiting for a place to stay,
I return there again,
into an inner smell
not outlined in pencil,
into a rounded cavity
where I am
a thin-legged schoolteacher,
where her vagina is clenched
like clenched teeth.

In this church with sagging entrails
a colored icon, cracked across the upper lip,
just above the sanctuary doorway,
and this church —
the schoolteacher is already dead.

COMMUNICATION

I am surprised at how dependent my feelings
are on blood pressure.
The electricity in my body does not let me sit still.
Still, I force myself not to move.

My fingers run nervously across the keyboard.
Then uneven texts turn into chimeras.

Your text messages follow me step for step.
And I do not want to be silent, yet I have nothing
to say to you.

The day is lost, and no pill can bring it back.
After it remains only an unpleasant fatigue.
Night — and an anxious sleep that cannot be
remembered.

It seems to me that I am happy,
feeling your warm closeness
and your fingers nearby.
Oh, these days, groundless like my poems,
intoxicate me with alcohol.

The whole day today is morning.
Cold drizzle, drops hanging in the air.
An empty autumn space.

It seems to me that I am happy beside you,
for I have never felt so confident and calm.
I hesitate whether everything is truly so good,
but when these days pass,
I think I will remember them
as the best.

— Close your eyes and relax, do you feel it?
— We have autumn with melancholy.
— This is just a temporary crisis of mine...

OLENA BORYSHPOLETS

(b. 1980) is a poet and artist from Odesa. Her poetry reflects the experience of displacement, civilian survival, and the fragmentation of everyday life under military threat. Writing across Ukrainian and diasporic spaces, she often situates intimate family memory within broader historical rupture.

Her poems combine documentary clarity with understated surreal shifts, focusing on war, exile, language, motherhood, and the persistence of private life amid catastrophe. She has left Ukraine since the full-scale invasion of 2022.

DOES YOUR CITY HAVE ENOUGH BIRDS

Does your city have enough birds?
Everyone has the right to ignore them.
A blind man feels the sun over his head
without any birds' words.
What is it all about, and where have they landed,
those damn birds?
The deaf man notices lost things and bodies —
there was a wall here,
and it's gone.
Why did we look at
that living rib?
So how many birds live in the city?

MY BROTHER' S RABBITS

When he slaughtered the rabbits,
the Russians were already bombing us.
We were cleaning up the basement of our relatives
because we didn't have a basement.
And Mom said:
I'm not going anywhere.
Not to anybody else's basement.
The day they shot
the first saboteurs in the neighborhood,
we carried carpets,
old furniture, warm clothes for the children.
Gunfire.
Gunfire.
Gunfire.
What is this? little Hlib asked me.
AKs, I said.
Oh! answered little Hlib,
and carried the garbage out of the basement.
The rabbits were still alive then,
and we were decorating the basement
in a desperate way.
And Mom said:
no basement.
She stayed in our house without a basement.
She wouldn't stay in the basement.
It must have been
when we were in the basement,
because the sirens were chasing us out of the house
like a frightened little pack.

Yeah, I think it was right then,
when we got the basement all set up.

He slaughtered the rabbits.

Every last one of them,
in a house he had been building himself
for the last ten years.

He knocked on his wife's
window at the clinic.
It was not a day off.

You cut the rabbits.

She said quietly.

Yes, I did. All of them.

She had seen him in his uniform
a long time ago,
before they had a son and a daughter,
before he built their house by himself.

His son has never eaten rabbit meat.

He really, really likes rabbits.

SHE HASN'T SEEN HER CAT IN SIX MONTHS

She hasn't seen her cat in six months,
but she has hope:
he reads her posts on social media.

She hasn't seen her mother in six months,
but she has hope:
she reads her posts on social media.

She hasn't seen Odesa in six months,
but she has hope:
she reads her posts on social media.

She hasn't seen the country in six months,

she

hasn't seen her home in six months,
hasn't seen her sisters in six months,
hasn't seen her friends in six months,
hasn't seen her brother in six months,
hasn't seen herself in six months.

She has hope.

SIX POLISH GIRLS ON A TRAIN

Six Polish girls on a train
across from me —
they don't know where I'm going.
I think they're going home.

The sound of the wheels energizes them.
Don't stop the train.
I can feel their laughter
that won't go away —
it crashes into my chest,
my knees, my elbows, my stomach.

The six Polish girls on the train
turn into my female family,
scrolling through their phones,
holding their school passes.

Don't count the nights,
not even the days.

One of them says
the man who fell asleep by the window is funny —
that's my grandmother, with a pink bow in her hair.
Another says to listen only to her,
and that's my grandmother too,
and she knows what she's talking about,
even in her sleep.
The third is warm and tired —
she doesn't like trains
at all. This is my mom.
I love you, third.
And I look:

the fourth is talking to someone
no one can see — and he answers her.
My sister, who hugs the fifth and the sixth,
and the name flies around the carriage.

Six Polish girls on a train.
The next stop is mine.

MY MOM SAID

My mom said: tomorrow the war will end.
That was a week ago.

I say: Don't leave the house.
Tell me how tired you are,
about the cat sleeping on your stomach,
about the seven raspberry bushes,
about Bohdan digging the garden,
about the neighbors' well
and the water that came out of it —
look for me.

I know nothing else, my dear,
but to listen to our abyss.
And yet there are still songs
that take the breath away.
February stops,
the mind stops,
the foreign air is the same as ours, Mom.
Strangers fill us up
so that we can be and listen.

We are told not to return to Ukraine
from Poland, from America,
from Norway, from Britain,
from Portugal, from France,
from Sweden, from the Czech Republic,
from Spain, from Denmark — especially from
Germany — not to return.

God, you're ugly.
We'll never kiss.

UKRAINIAN CHILDREN

Ukrainian children around the world
are going to schools —
the living Ukrainian children;
the dead go to graves.

In foreign countries
the sun sets on children's skin,
foreign birds peck at their memory and faith,
a foreign language grows warm like a blanket
on which life depends.
This winter they will not return.
Let them sleep peacefully, just for a while.
Who will fly over next spring?
Who will fall and say:

Let's stay here,
where the birds and the sun are —
let them peck.

The yellow tree
covers the roots with leaves.
If there are words in the world,
they are foreign.

If there is a past,
it is only grass now.
Children are alive on the grass,
children under the grass —
those who are gone.

ORPHEUS AND EURYDICE IN NEW YORK

When street names are just numbers,
they won't be renamed
if the country's government changes,
or the language of the country, or if it snows
heavily.

Far away from here, where the war is going on,
people are changing the names of streets
to the names of Ukrainian heroes
who will never walk those streets.

South St, Sea St, Milky Way St,
Independence-from-Hopes Beach,
Freedom-of-Action-in-Complete-Darkness Street...
Tell the truth, change the rules,
interfere with history,
stay alive,
don't look back.

Jade said she didn't want children.
I said I couldn't give birth.
He said he was fine.

And then Jade asked me
if I was afraid of being a writer.

I am not afraid.

On Broadway, he and I saw Orpheus and Eurydice.
Orpheus looked back, and at that moment I closed
my eyes.

You're never going to see her again, you fool.
But he knew it — everyone knows it.

And we moved on,
not because we wanted to, but because
we couldn't help them.

The three days of the storm in New York tested
our minds,
our bodies, our story.
The helpless feeling of being little children
never left me for a minute.
At least we are all really somebody's child —
even Orpheus.

I wish my father had held me by the shoulders
at least once in the wind,
like in Louise Glück's poem "Snow,"
where she escapes the heavy snow
engulfing New York City
through the miracle of her father's arms.
Just once.

I like numbers.
I like to walk.
Don't look back, just don't look back —
these two can still be helped.

MY MOTHER DANCES

My mother dances in our house
in the Ukrainian village of Hildendorf,
which is the old name of a German colony
whose inhabitants disappeared
during the Second World War.
Now the village has a different name, different
inhabitants, and a different war.

Once, a German woman named Ira and I
went to visit the old German graves.
On the cemetery stones from the twentieth century
it was almost impossible to read the names,
so Ira picked up a handful of cemetery grass
and started rubbing it on the old stones.
Fragrant letters and numbers flew into the air,
because the herb she was rubbing on the stones
was arugula.

Damn, Ira, it's arugula! —
I screamed into the dead silence,
and at that same moment thunder
rolled over the estuary.
Ira was taking pictures of the fragrant inscriptions,
and a thunderstorm began.
Ira's grandmother was deported
from Ukraine to Kazakhstan
during the Soviet era;
maybe she was afraid of thunderstorms too,
maybe she was not afraid of anything.

When we ran through the cemetery to the exit,
water was already pouring down from the sky
like a flood,

and it washed away the inscriptions we had
brought to life for five minutes,
and the stones went numb again.
Lightning did not strike us in the Ukrainian steppe.
We were running away from the cemetery, and Ira
was screaming through the flood:
I am afraid, I am very afraid of thunderstorms!

Ira returned to Germany.
We hugged goodbye
until the first happy tear.
Six months later, the Russians were already
bombing Hildendorf,
and the first saboteurs were coming from the side
of the estuary, not far from the cemetery.
And my mother, my mother — she would turn on
the music and dance every day.
It's a kind of whim.
She is also afraid of thunderstorms.

THE GYPSY

The gypsy woman picks up a carp by the gills with two fingers
and hides it in the abyss of her skirt.
A fish caught by the head
whips the air and the bright fabric with its tail
and continues to live in the strong hands of its new owner.
In the trough from which it was taken,
other carps wave their flapping tails at her.
Not only people like to say goodbye.

I bought some meat that day,
in the old market stalls
where I used to sell vegetables with my grandma.
I called her Bulia, because I loved her.
She had seen a lot in her life: revolution, war, famine,
my drunken grandfather,
the black soil and the market.

So we used to sell dill, onions,
garlic, cherries, and fragrant
apricots by the bucketful.
Those apricots were legendary among buyers,
those cherries were the size of someone's heart.

I was small, and the market felt like home.
To earn good money,
Bulia and I had to wake up at five in the morning.
Bulia is long gone.
I still love sunrises
more than anything else in my life.

At the market,
I was stung by a wasp for the first time,
between the fingers of my right hand,
and my hand swelled so much
it looked like a flipper.
And then I thought,
after Bulia told me
to go to the stinking market toilet
and pee on the place where I was bitten
so it wouldn't hurt:

It would be nice to have fins.

The pain did not stop.

Oh, God, oh, God!
That first day of a wasp sting
we earned a whole lot of money!
And Bulia bought me a sugar pretzel,
which was scary to eat —
it was so beautiful.

By the way, the gypsy's skirt,
in which she was hiding a huge
stolen carp with two fingers,
which, in its wavy, sea-like fabric,
was wagging its tail at us all as it was saying
goodbye —
that skirt was mesmerizing.

And I, already an adult, stopped
in the middle of the market and stood there.
People were in a hurry to buy dill, onions, garlic,
cherries and other people's apricots.
They passed by me.

I wish the carp seller had seen
how the gypsy woman creates her everyday art,
how the carp flies around in her skirt around her hips.

Here is one of my stories,
about a fish dinner for a gypsy family.
Bulia wanted to swim in the sea before she died.
That market still exists in Odesa today.

INVITATION

It will fly and land on thc roof —
that loud helicopter.
It took me six months to learn
not to be afraid of that sound,
but people stronger than me say
that in difficult times you
shouldn't talk about your fears.

One day, non-military aircraft
will return to the Ukrainian sky,
but for now I see you running
to take a picture of the Allegheny rescue helicopter.

When you come to these rivers, to these hills,
to these endless Pittsburgh rains,
the wind licks you with a metal bar
and sprinkles you with metal dust
and invites you to the steelworkers' museum
and gives you a ticket to the red-hot furnace
and tells you how hot it's going to be
and tells you how much it will hurt
and how you'll be blinded
and how you won't be able to do anything
and how you'll be melted in the end

and how you'll feel life
when it sits down next to you,
when it speaks
with a ticket in your hand.

God, you run
to get that shot
as if you were the salvation.

You can't — you can't love anymore.

The helicopter from Allegheny Hospital
lands on the rescue roof,
and I take out my phone to take a picture of you.

FROM THE SHORE

You can't see me from the shore,
I float away like time,
where all the living say to the dead:
wait for us.

Black sea, black clouds,
the earth smells black,
young blond Neptune
is embracing the ships.

OLEH KOTSAREV

(b. 1981) is a poet, translator, and journalist associated with contemporary experimental and urban poetry. Born in Kharkiv, he emerged in the early 2000s as part of a generation that expanded Ukrainian poetic language through irony, visual composition, and attention to everyday urban landscapes.

His work often explores the intersection of ordinary life and historical violence, combining documentary detail with subtle absurdity and linguistic play. After the full-scale Russian invasion of Ukraine in 2022, Kotsarev remained in Bucha.

GRAY SLIDE

choosing what to photograph
For Foreigners —
which of the two children's slides
pockmarked by fragments of russia
that children still slide down

it's easy to see
that the yellow spiral plastic one
fits much better than
the flat metal gray one

color intrigue catharsis what can you say

so of course we will photograph
it

sorry, gray slide,
you were unlucky today
you know yourself,
gray slide —
it's not that we are like this,
it's just life like this

STATION: MATCHBOX

Nothing good was there,
nothing special ever happened.

Walls like crossword puzzles of beige tile.
Curled seats in the cramped hall.
Wanted posters of legendary criminals.
A senseless customs desk.

The station —
a small matchbox
on the border.

A square cluttered with smugglers' goods —
butter, herring, sleepy human bodies.
Green benches, yellow conversations, a yellowed
rose of dialects.
Four windows on the façade, three on the sides.
A square dog: a parody of a portal.
The first symphony of squeaking bicycles.
A bus resembling a grandmother.
No, this is not a poetic comparison:
the grandmother was gone — and the bus was
gone.

And all this once or twice a day.
Otherwise — just cold and warm silence.
Grumbling knotweed among the rust of rails.

A place-about-nothing. A Great History of Nothing.
After N sister explosions here — only another
installation
of broken matches.

So why after explosion N+1,
shown in a new silent film
[reincarnation of the genre]
"An explosive drone arrives at the railway station,"
did it hurt more than
after all the other ruins —
buildings more spectacular or more integrated
into the nervous system and the swamps of
memory?

Oh! On the platform
that night
there was
an earthen toad!

BEACH

on our Desna —
— the river that in its calm
has rejected balance,
has rejected dialectics:
at once swift and wide —
on our Desna,
on the beach, for two years now,
fragments of an explosion,
participants of the explosion,
insects of the explosion,
have peppered the changing booths.

look through these small openings —
how mysterious in them
bare human bodies seem,
moving as if water
behind a wall shaped like a river.

SKIPPED AIR RAID SIREN

1.we run with our five-year-old daughter
down from the fifth floor,
and for a moment it becomes funny:
our legs dangle in the air,
we truly touch
only each other,
astronauts,
cosmonauts.

2. you start skipping
air raid sirens
like a high school student.

3. who moves
in the dark building
across from your dark building —
the building
in which
your dark hair
stirred?

6. a refugee plays
unfairly —
in his sleeves
there are eight words
from different
dialects.

BEST DAYS

"Grandma, what was it like for you
under the occupation?"

"Oh, it was hard, sonny —
I barely survived."

"And when ours came back,
did it get easier?"

"Easier, but not really:
people flooded in,
everything got expensive,
repairs everywhere."

"When was it good for you then?"

"The best time was
after those bastards had already fled
and ours still hadn't come —
quiet, peaceful,
no one around."

And she gave me an apple
and hobbled off
across the railway tracks,
past the portrait of Shurik the dog,
killed during the fighting.

And I went to the park.
It was cold — mid-autumn, rain —
but in the bushes
a cricket was singing.
Or whatever you call it.

ALINA DANYLOVA

(b. 2000) is a poet and cultural manager from Mykolaiv, Ukraine. She describes herself through a constellation of vivid, personal markers that echo the tone of her writing — intimate, ironic, and quietly defiant.

Danylova also speaks of assembling her own "bi-combo": bipolar, bisexual, bilingual. Through her writing she seeks to expand visibility and empathy, emphasizing that no label determines a person's human or professional value.

She likes to note that when she was eleven, an owl lived in her home for several months — which she considers unofficial confirmation that she had been admitted to Hogwarts.

Since Russia's full-scale invasion of Ukraine in 2022, she moved to Berlin, Germany.

DEATH AND LOVE

zoomers will think of robots.
i'm thinking of cyberpunk and clean gin in clubs on the far side.

millennials will probably think of Scarlett O'Hara.
i'm thinking — what is that?

i started reading *Emmanuel* but grew up halfway.
in my hometown they say:
everybody jerks off however they want.
that's Dush,
my mother's language.
and my father, you know —
a pirate, still holding onto his charisma.

did you know bees die in the winter?
sounds like the beginning of some vanilla poem
about the romanticization of war and the new Executed Renaissance.

time moves, conversations move — people don't.
someone's stuck,
alive and holding on.
someone's making it through.
i'm jealous.

youth sewn into holes in jacket pockets.
now it's sustainable:
bio into bio,
plastic into plastic,
paper into paper,
rockets rockets rockets rockets.

sleep curls into the bend of his hip,
in the half-closed feeling of light
when you're flying downhill
and screaming —

whether from grief
or
from love.

ABOUT THE TRANSLATOR

Oleksandr Frazé-Frazénko (b. 1989) is a filmmaker, writer, translator, and musician from Halychyna. His work spans poetry, prose, documentary film, and literary translation. He is the author of the English-language novel Nothing Is Under Control and the poetry collection FAQ Ukraine, as well as numerous books in Ukrainian. He was the first to translate and publish the poetry of Jim Morrison in Ukrainian. His translation of Olena Boryshpolets' Orpheus and Eurydice in New York was shortlisted for the Derek Walcott Prize for Poetry. He is a member of PEN America.

As a filmmaker, he is known for poetic documentaries about major Ukrainian cultural figures, including Chubai (2014); The House on Seven Winds (2015), about Vasyl Makhno; An Aquarium in the Sea (2016), about the New York Group of Poets; Malaniuk (2019); and A Song for M (2022), about Bohdan Rubchak.

He is co-founder of the independent press OFF Laboratory, which publishes and translates contemporary Ukrainian literature. A recipient of grants from the National Endowment for the Arts and the Heinz Endowments, in collaboration with RealTime Arts. He produces music and performs with his wife, Mari Frazé-Frazénko, as Ceramic Knives.

www.ingramcontent.com/pod-product-compliance
Lightning Source LLC
LaVergne TN
LVHW090524110826
845146LV00003B/970